Take Off!

Your Pocket Coach to Student Success
An Interactive Journal

PEACEFUL VIKING BOOKS

Émile Odbäck Nelson
Åsa Filippa Odbäck

Copyright © 2016 Émile Nelson & Åsa Odbäck

Printed in the United States
Book Design by Émile Nelson
Cover Design by Åsa Odbäck & Émile Nelson

ISBN: 978-0692776063

First Published in the United States of America by Peaceful Viking Books, 2016

About the Authors:

Émile Odbäck Nelson recently graduated from UC Santa Barbara as a member of Phi Beta Kappa with straight As, Highest Honors and a University Award of Distinction. He also delivered the graduation speech. During his time at UCSB, he conducted research in English and Writing, worked for a Hollywood Director and served as Editor in Chief for UCSB's nationally ranked newspaper.

PEACEFUL VIKING.COM

Åsa Filippa Odbäck graduated #1 in her class from Law School, after which she taught law at the University of Stockholm before proceeding to again graduate #1 from Stockholm Business School. She then founded a major success training firm that worked with international companies like Volvo and Ericsson. Later, she served as head of Press and Information for the Swedish Minister of Defense before moving to California where she has been an author and a painter. Most recently, her art was shown in Los Angeles, Stockholm and NYC.

To everyone who has helped us along the way:

Thank you!

Welcome to
Your Pocket Coach!

Everyone needs a coach, but not everyone could afford one… Until now.

Why do college students need a coach?

– Less than 35% of students graduate in four years

– The average six-year graduation rate is 60%

– Of students who start, 40% never graduate college

– Antidepressant use is up 400% from 1988

– College students are 50% more likely to abuse "study drugs" than their non-college counterparts

– 80 Million Americans report not even having one friend

It's not easy to be a student!
That's what *Your Pocket Coach* is for.

Your Pocket Coach delivers the benefits of a personal coach at a fraction of the cost of actually having one. We have condensed the wisdom of a combined total of 12 years of straight-A college and post-grad experience, along with almost a decade of university teaching experience, into 160 pages of interactive, easy-to-use lessons designed to show you how to be the best possible student and person that you can be.

Your Pocket Coach is the ideal mix between a book (to deliver information) and a journal (to help you digest and understand the information.) This also means that, in addition to world-class coaching, this book delivers the well-documented and wide-reaching benefits of journaling ⟶

> *Boosted IQ, better memory, expanded creativity, improved problem solving, increased mental clarity, reduced stress, a much higher chance of reaching your goals and more.*

With thought experiments and prompts throughout the entire book, Your Pocket Coach actively engages you every step of the way, ensuring that you learn and understand – rather than read and forget – something new every time you work with it.

"A personal journal is an ideal environment in which to 'become.' It is a perfect place for you to think, feel, discover, expand, remember, and dream."

Brad Wilcox

How Does This Work?

As we create this guidebook together, your job is to interact with the words we've already put in. When you feel inspired to write, draw, think and hopefully act, we ask that you just do it!

These pages pass no judgment, so we ask that you be as honest, open and forthcoming as possible as you work through it. Your Pocket Coach is only here to help, and we are certain that it will.

> "LIFE IS REALLY SIMPLE, BUT WE
> INSIST ON MAKING IT COMPLICATED."
> CONFUCIUS

We recommend that you try to get into a rhythm of working with Your Pocket Coach, so we suggest setting aside 15-20 minutes per day to interact with it. You are obviously not being graded on this, so feel free to do whatever you feel like! Just remember, like most things in life, you get out what you put in.

We also ask that you keep your copy private to ensure you have total freedom to express yourself however you want!

Enjoy the Ride!

Margaret Hons
_____
(SIGN YOUR NAME HERE — CLAIM OWNERSHIP!)
This is my Pocket Coach!

If found, please return to:

Margaret Hons

Reward for returned book: a thorough thank you and a hearty high five!

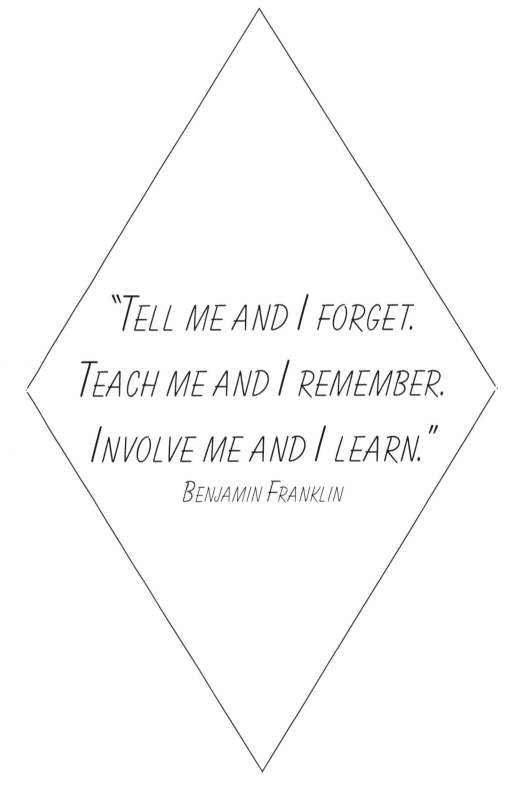

"Tell me and I forget.
Teach me and I remember.
Involve me and I learn."
Benjamin Franklin

Your Pocket Coach is designed to keep you involved every step of the way so you can learn and understand as much as possible. Please write, draw, color, and scribble all over it!

Whenever you see a prompt, use it for inspiration, but let your mind take you where it will. There are no right or wrong answers. Try it right here:

WHAT ARE YOU HOPING TO GET OUT OF COLLEGE? WHAT ARE YOU INTERESTED TO LEARN? WHERE DO YOU WANT TO GO FROM HERE?

Make the Switch!

On September 2, 1967 all of Sweden drove on the left side of the road, as they had always done. On September 3, the country awoke and, suddenly, everyone had to drive on the right. In one single night, the entire country changed from driving on the left, to driving on the right.

A reasonable guess would be that it was a dark and bloody day for the country, with car parts flying every which direction as people struggled to figure out how to change everything they knew about driving. But that guess would be totally off.

During the first Monday after the change, the amount of accidents actually fell below the average Monday accident rate, and for the next six weeks, accidents dropped 40 percent.

———————————————

One day, you wake up and everything has changed from what you're used to... You're in college! Now you have the chance to change into the person you've always wanted to be, but might have thought it was impossible to become. But, if you implement a few of the principles from Your Pocket coach, you, too, can make a seemingly impossible change and become a huge success.

> "THE LAW OF WIN-WIN SAYS,
> LET'S NOT DO IT YOUR WAY OR MY WAY;
> LET'S DO IT THE BEST WAY."
> GREG ANDERSON

How do you succeed in college?
In short, do what the Swedes did.

1. Work with change, not against it!
2. Cooperate with your peers!
3. Be focused and present!
4. Be ready for accidents - yours and others'!
5. Avoid being dragged into someone else's accident!
6. Have empathy, forgiveness and compassion for those around you who, like you, are learning!
7. Set an example!

These seven principles are much more than just ideas about how to switch from driving on one side to the other. Together, they provide a proven foundation for performing and living at your best.

It's Your Pocket Coach's job to show you how to excel in college, and have a great time doing it, all by following these basic ideas.

Your Pocket Coach combines the Swedish community-oriented ideals with the American philosophy of personal excellence to deliver you the best possible pieces of each culture. In doing so, Your Pocket Coach can help you learn how to not only be an outstanding student, but also how to live a successful, rewarding life in school and after.

August 10, 1628

All of Stockholm watched as the most fearsome, awe-inspiring ship of the century, the Swedish pride and joy — the Vasa — slowly set out to sea for its maiden voyage. Cheers of national pride and celebration rang out from the city as the sails raised and billowed with wind. But one powerful gust changed all of that.

Cheers and celebration turned to chaos and panic as the enormous sails, now tasting wind for the first time, violent pushed the unprepared Vasa onto its side. As water flowed in through the cannon ports and the crew abandoned ship, Stockholm watched their country's flagship sink to a premature watery grave.

So the most beautiful ship in the world lay underwater for hundreds of years, stuck in the very port from which it launched. Why? Because the builders made the ship so beautiful and awesome that they forget to even make it seaworthy.

In the end, it took much more money, time and effort to rescue the ship from the bottom of the sea than it would have taken to simply make it right the first time. Still, the ship still will never sail. Instead, it is one of the grandest relics of all time; fated to sit in a museum forever.

Don't be a Grand Relic!

When we focus too much on beauty and appearance, an unexpected wind can be all it takes to sink us.

Many of us focus so much on looking good and impressing people, but just like the Vasa, without the proper foundation, even the most impressive-looking student is only a gust away from sinking.

College is about preparing yourself to actually be ready when you set sail into the "real world," so you don't end up a relic, yourself.

If you work with Your Pocket Coach you will learn how to not only be ready for just about anything college can throw at you, but also how to look good and have a great time doing it. It will teach you how to be good, so you can look good. Not the other way around.

Don't be like the Vasa; prepare yourself for success — as a student and in life — with Your Pocket Coach.

"Be a yardstick of quality. Some people aren't used to an environment where excellence is expected."
STEVE JOBS

WHAT GETS YOU PUMPED ABOUT COLLEGE?
WHAT AWESOME EXPERIENCES DO YOU HOPE TO HAVE?
WHAT COOL STUFF DO YOU WANT TO LEARN?

Keep your head in the clouds

WHAT ARE YOU HOPING TO ACCOMPLISH IN YOUR TIME HERE?
WHO DO YOU WANT TO BE FOUR YEARS FROM NOW?
WHAT ARE SOME OF YOUR PLANS?
WHAT ARE YOUR GOALS?

NICE SHOES!

Keep your feet on the ground

Nervous is just another word for

Pumped!

You're here! That means you are already a success! Over 93% of people in the world never make it to college. You should be very proud of what you've already accomplished. And, guess what? Your success is only going to keep building from here. Congratulate yourself! You deserve it.

> "ALL WORTHWHILE MEN HAVE GOOD THOUGHTS, GOOD IDEAS AND GOOD INTENTIONS – BUT PRECIOUS FEW OF THEM EVER TRANSLATE THOSE INTO ACTION."
> JOHN HANCOCK

WHAT DID YOU DO TO CREATE THIS SUCCESS? LIST A FEW THINGS, HABITS, ROUTINES AND PEOPLE THAT HAVE HELPED YOU GET HERE.

I AM SUCCESSFUL BECAUSE...

Don't worry if you don't feel perfectly confident right away. Everybody in college is nervous for one reason or another. Some people are terrified to move away from home, leave their friends, change their routines, meet new people, etc. etc.

> "KEEP ON GOING AND THE CHANCES ARE YOU WILL STUMBLE ON SOMETHING, PERHAPS WHEN YOU ARE LEAST EXPECTING IT. I HAVE NEVER HEARD OF ANYONE STUMBLING ON SOMETHING SITTING DOWN."
> CHARLES KETTERING

Let the nerves come out. Talk about them with the people around you. I guarantee you that you're not the only one feeling whatever it is you're feeling. Everybody is unique, sure, but not that unique.

Use your emotions
(happy or sad)
to connect to others!

Shared sorrow is half sorrow —

What are some emotions that you're feeling right now? why? Try to fill the page!

Shared happiness is double happiness.

THE FUNDAMENTALS

1: *Your health — mental and physical — comes first.*
Nothing else matters if you don't have your health. If you ever feel overwhelmed, scared, out of control or even just sad, please reach out to somebody. There are professionals at every school who only want to help in times of struggle.

2: *Be kind to yourself and others.*
If you find yourself falling out of kindness, you're not on the right track.

Be kind to your parents, too. They're probably just as nervous as you are about you going to college. Give them a break if they act a little strange; you're their baby and this can be a very scary time for them, too.

3: *Remove yourself from any situation where people do not treat you with respect.*
Anyone who treats you with anything less than respect is not someone you want to call your boss, coworker, brother, sister, lover or even friend. If someone doesn't treat you with respect from day one, that is not someone you want to associate yourself with, regardless of how popular or successful he/she might seem.

4: *Treat every situation as an opportunity to learn.*
An attitude of constant learning, from positive and negative situations will put you miles ahead of your peers.

*A*DD YOUR OWN RULES TO LIVE BY, IN COLLEGE & BEYOND.

1.

2.

3.

4.

fIRST...

If you want to perform at a level above the average, you need to first become a person that is above average. Much of this book, even if it doesn't seem to directly influence your academics, is designed to make you the best student and person that you can be. By improving yourself, your mind and your life choices, you are building the foundation for your success in scholarship, leadership and friendship — so you won't become a sinking ship, like the Vasa.

> "ALL MY LIFE, I ALWAYS WANTED TO BE SOMEBODY. NOW I SEE THAT I SHOULD HAVE BEEN MORE SPECIFIC."
> JANE WAGNER

WHAT COULD BE YOUR WEAKNESSES AND LIMITATIONS IN COLLEGE?
HOW CAN YOU PREPARE YOURSELF TO BEST ADDRESS THEM?

Knowing yourself is the first step toward improving yourself.

15

Give it All You've Got!
Be the best you that you can be

"If a man is called to be a street sweeper, he should sweep streets even as a Michelangelo painted, or Beethoven composed music or Shakespeare wrote poetry. He should sweep streets so well that all the hosts of heaven and earth will pause to say, 'Here lived a great street sweeper who did his job well.'"

Martin Luther King Jr.

ARE YOU DOING YOUR VERY BEST RIGHT NOW?

IS THERE A WAY YOU COULD DO IT EVEN BETTER?

WHAT'S STOPPING YOU?

Be Nice!
To Yourself

Give yourself what you need! You can't rely on other people to make you feel loved, appreciated, validated, etc. If you don't feel it inside, you'll never be satisfied with what other people can give you. So, treat yourself how you'd want your perfect best friend to treat you.

"It's not selfish to love yourself, take care of yourself, and to make your happiness a priority. It's necessary."
Mandy Hale

WRITE YOURSELF A LETTER, LISTING ALL THE THINGS YOU REALLY APPRECIATE ABOUT YOURSELF. LEAVE OUT THE BUTS, IFS, ETC. TRY TO KEEP IT ALL POSITIVE ALL THE WAY THROUGH!

You are a magnet: you attract what you focus on.
If you want things to improve, focus on the good in
yourself and others.

When you do something right,
appreciate yourself for it!

I APPRECIATE THAT I...

When you do something wrong,
learn from it. Then appreciate yourself for it!

1 APPRECIATE THAT 1 LEARNED....

End of story:
Be your own best friend.

> "*I'M NOT PARTICULARLY NEEDY, AND I'M NOT PARTICULARLY ANXIOUS. I DON'T LOOK FOR A DIRECTOR TO TELL ME I'M DOING A GOOD JOB OR THAT I'M GREAT. I DON'T NEED TO BE STROKED. IT'S MORE MY OWN YARDSTICK.*"
> CATE BLANCHETT

When you feel good about what you do, your self-confidence improves, and confidence is one of the single most important characteristics of successful people. So be kind to yourself and others and you will not only find yourself feeling more self confident, but more successful, too!

WRITE A SHORT NOTE EACH NIGHT APPRECIATING 3 THINGS YOU DID DURING THAT DAY. THESE COULD BE SMALL THINGS, LIKE WAKING UP ON TIME, EATING HEALTHY OR COMPLETING AN ASSIGNMENT. TO GET IN THE SWING OF THINGS, TRY TO LIST SOME OF YOUR BIGGEST AND BEST ACCOMPLISHMENTS TO DATE RIGHT HERE!

How can a regular chain tied around a little wooden post hold a 6000lb elephant?

As a baby, they chained that elephant to the post. The more it struggled, the deeper the chain cut it. Eventually it would stop struggling. Even when it grew to a size where it could rip that post out of the ground without a second thought, it would not struggle against the chain that caused it so much pain. It "knew" there was no point in fighting. It had learned that it was helpless and that trying was **hopeless.**

WHAT ARE THE CHAINS THAT HOLD YOU BACK?

.

HAVE FUN WITH FEAR

When we get scared, we become less intelligent and less able to distinguish between real danger and fear. This means that we interpret any uncertainty as real danger, when the vast majority of the time, it's just emotion or a thought – just fear. We get caught up in our heads and we resort to instinct: fight, flight or freeze.

> *"FEAR IS THE ENEMY OF LOGIC. THERE IS NO MORE DEBILITATING, SELF-DEFEATING, SICKENING THING IN THE WORLD — TO AN INDIVIDUAL OR TO A NATION."*
> *FRANK SINATRA*

Learning most often involves some type of falling down, and you can either suffer from it or learn from it! Mistakes are your stepping stones to excellence.

> *"THE GREATEST MISTAKE YOU CAN MAKE IN LIFE IS TO BE CONTINUALLY FEARING YOU WILL MAKE ONE."*
> *ELBERT HUBBARD*

WHAT ARE YOUR WORST FEARS? WHY? WHAT WOULD YOU DO DIFFERENTLY IF YOU COULD OVERCOME THEM? WHAT'S THE WORST THAT COULD HAPPEN IF YOU FACED THEM?

Take Care of Your Body!

It Should Last a Lifetime

If you're feeling down, a little bit of exercise helps shake off bad moods and extra pounds. Many of the most successful people in the world point to exercise as one of their most important habits because it gives them more energy than it takes. And studies have even shown that exercise is sometimes more effective than antidepressants at treating depression.

> "PHYSICAL FITNESS IS NOT ONLY ONE OF THE MOST IMPORTANT KEYS TO A HEALTHY BODY, IT IS THE BASIS OF DYNAMIC AND CREATIVE INTELLECTUAL ACTIVITY."
> JOHN F. KENNEDY

At the very least, make sure to get up out of your chair as often as you can remember! Some experts say sitting is the new smoking; it contributes to several diseases and can shorten your life. So get up out of your chair every once in a while and help yourself stay alive!

Tracking your exercise, eating and drinking habits always leads to improvement. As you increase your focus on these things, you will notice that you begin to make better choices for yourself.

"FOOD IS AN IMPORTANT PART OF A BALANCED DIET."

Fran Lebowitz

WHAT IS YOUR PLAN TO TAKE CARE OF YOUR BODY DURING COLLEGE? WHAT ARE YOU DOING THAT WORKS? AND WHAT HABITS COULD YOU IMPROVE? WHAT IS ONE SMALL CHANGE THAT YOU COULD MAKE?

"I COULDN'T HELP IT. I CAN RESIST EVERYTHING, EXCEPT TEMPTATION."

Oscar Wilde

Give Yourself a Break!

Many people struggle to take breaks because they feel they're a waste of time, but part of creating a balanced life is giving yourself a break. When we push ourselves to work long hours without breaks, we do not work efficiently. **The brain needs breaks to convert information into memory,** and when we don't give the brain those breaks, we get bored and distracted and start to waste time on other things.

> *"I'm trying not to put too much pressure on myself, but I think I'm overcompensating. I'm putting too much pressure on myself to not put too much pressure on myself."*
>
> Dan Bilardello

Productivity skyrockets when the brain feels stimulated, relaxed and engaged. And the best way to keep your brain happy is to take a break, stretch out and connect with something or someone else! When you get back at it, you and your brain are open and ready to get new ideas, new perspectives and complete the task much easier and faster.

Try This! Every 20 minutes, stand up, stretch like a yawning cat and reach your hands up to the ceiling, take a few deep breaths (focus on your exhales) and refocus your eyes on something far away. This 20-second pause makes a huge difference for your mind and your body – it's like rebooting yourself!

30

WRITE ONE LONG, UNINTERRUPTED SENTENCE ABOUT WHY YOU
DON'T HAVE TIME TO TAKE CARE OF YOURSELF, EXERCISE, SLEEP, EAT
HEALTHY, WRITE IN YOUR JOURNAL, TAKE BREAKS, ETC.

NO PUNCTUATION MARKS OF ANY KIND! NO BREAKS!
JUST PUSH THROUGH UNTIL YOU FILL THE PAGE.

"WE WILL BE MORE SUCCESSFUL IN ALL OUR ENDEAVORS IF WE CAN LET GO OF
THE HABIT OF RUNNING ALL THE TIME, AND TAKE LITTLE PAUSES TO RELAX AND
RE-CENTER OURSELVES. AND WE'LL ALSO HAVE A LOT MORE JOY IN LIVING."
THICH NHAT HANH

Usually, when we work without breaks it's very hard to keep focused on the original task. Unexpected things often steal our attention from what we set out to do.

HOW CAN YOU MAKE TIME FOR BREAKS THAT WILL MOTIVATE AND REWARD YOU, AND ALSO REBOOT YOUR SYSTEM? WHAT ARE SOME EXAMPLES OF THESE KINDS OF SHORT BREAKS?

Take breaks to get a breakthrough!
Breaks Boost Your...
Productivity!
Focus!
Learning!
Memory!
Creativity & problem solving!
General wellbeing!

Fika
The Swedish Secret to Success

Fika is the Swedish tradition of taking breaks and connecting with one-other over a cup of coffee and some snacks. To have Fika, sit down with a group of friends, turn off all cellphones and computers and share some nice coffee, snacks and conversation.Just be present and connect with your Fika partners!

Fika is not just about the coffee. Fika is about taking a real break (even 10/15 minutes) and spending time with another real person — another human, not a phone or TV.

Studies show how much more productive and motivated we are when we have a group of some sort to keep us on track, and Fika presents you with a group of people who are there to both support you and be supported by you to get out and succeed.

Taking short breaks to laugh and relax with friends improves your ability to solve problems and find new creative solutions. Chances are that every day you use something the Swedes developed between fika breaks: Spotify, Skype, GPS, seatbelts, zippers, flat screen monitors, energy saving light bulbs, etc. etc.

34

If you want to be successful, surround yourself with people who have similar goals and can push you to constantly improve.

> "IF YOU ARE THE SMARTEST PERSON IN THE ROOM, YOU
> ARE IN THE WRONG ROOM."
> ANONYMOUS

Many of us get stuck in the "ugh" rut: Ugh! More work. Ugh! So much traffic. Ugh! What a long line. And unfortunately, when we're stuck down there, it can be almost impossible to get ourselves out. But when you have a Fika group or any group to help you back up, things often don't feel so "ugh," after all.

> "IF YOU HAVE ZEST AND ENTHUSIASM YOU ATTRACT ZEST
> AND ENTHUSIASM. LIFE DOES GIVE BACK IN KIND."
> NORMAN VINCENT PEALE

Who are some people you would like to invite to have coffee once a week? Start your own Fika group!

Be Lucky!

According to recent research, only 10% of luck is left to chance. You control the other 90% through things like your attitude, perspective, behavior. Basically, if you believe yourself to be lucky, you increase your chances of actually becoming lucky!

> "LUCK IS NOT A MAGICAL ABILITY OR A GIFT FROM THE GODS... INSTEAD, IT IS A WAY OF THINKING AND BEHAVING."
> DR. RICHARD WISEMAN

In short, one of the biggest "luck" studies showed that traditionally lucky people focus on the good in their lives, maintain positive relationships, smile often and actively seek opportunities around them. These habits **create** luck.

> *"I'M A GREAT BELIEVER IN LUCK AND I FIND THE HARDER I WORK THE MORE I HAVE OF IT."*
>
> THOMAS JEFFERSON

DO YOU CONSIDER YOURSELF LUCKY? WHY OR WHY NOT?

If you want to have more luck in your life, look for ways to make other people lucky!

It can be as easy as offering your seat on the bus to someone who looks tired, paying for someone's coffee behind you or picking up a treat for a friend - it's all about little things.

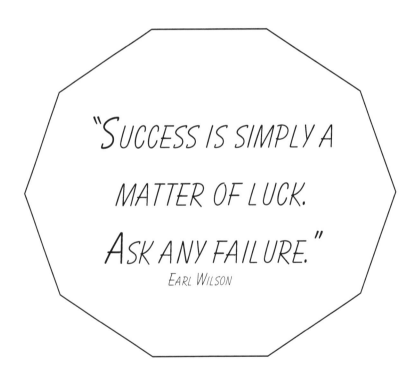

"SUCCESS IS SIMPLY A MATTER OF LUCK. ASK ANY FAILURE."
EARL WILSON

How can you be the reason someone feels lucky today?

"It is literally true, that you can succeed best and quickest by helping others to succeed."
Napoleon Hill

Surround yourself with people who believe themselves to be lucky, too. Their luck or lack thereof will inevitably rub off on you.

THERE'S AN OLD IDEA THAT YOU ARE THE AVERAGE OF THE 5 PEOPLE YOU SPEND THE MOST TIME WITH. WHO DOES THAT MAKE YOU? IS THAT WHO YOU WANT TO BE?

(I'm not saying I totally agree with this idea, but it is an interesting experiment to reflect on who you choose to spend your time with.)

Even beyond luck, if you have people around you who believe you to be awesome, you actually become more awesome.

In a famous experiment, a scientist had his assistants time rats as they navigated a maze. Without explaining why, the lead scientist randomly labeled half of the cages as "smart" and the other as "dumb."

Despite the fact that the assistants were under strict instructions to treat each rat exactly the same, the rats labeled "smart" completed the maze much faster than those who were labeled "dumb."

It wasn't that the half of the rats that were randomly selected and deemed smart were different than the others. It boils down to a difference in expectations and microscopic changes in handling and treatment that lead to big differences in results.

Still not convinced? Look up the Rosenthal Effect. Basically, teachers were told certain groups of randomly selected students were exceptional and others were below average, and each group performed according to the teachers' expectations.

Surround yourself with people who believe in you, and who you believe in, too. And please make sure you believe in yourself!

Make Yourself Proud
(of yourself)

A lot of us forget to take a look at ourselves and whether we like where we're at – life moves quickly and it's so easy to get swept up in the craziness and forget to check where we're heading. Keep an eye on what excuses you use as a crutch for why you are not doing what you want to be.

I'm going to ask you to do a quick reflection. And just be honest because, well… is anybody else here? Nope.

Please be gentle with yourself; this is not meant to make you depressed or disappointed, it's just a way to get some perspective.

This is your big chance to become someone you are proud of!

Thinking of yourself as a victim doesn't make you victorious.

ARE YOU PROUD OF YOURSELF, WHAT YOU'VE ACCOMPLISHED,
WHO YOU ARE AND WHAT YOU'RE DOING?
IF SO, WHY? IF NOT, WHAT DO YOU NEED TO CHANGE?

Have

Fun!

Optimize Your Attitude!

An old man told his grandson, "There are two wolves inside all of us, battling to the death — one good and one evil. The good wolf fights for happiness, loving, acceptance, enthusiasm, creativity and generosity. The evil wolf fights for fear, hatred, discrimination, violence, greed and negativity."

"So which wolf wins?" The boy asked.

"Whichever one you feed." The grandfather said. "Whichever one you feed…"

WHICH WOLF DO YOU FEED?
WHICH WOLF DO THE PEOPLE AROUND YOU FEED?

Changing your attitude, even about the small, daily things, like waiting in line, can change your whole day and your whole life.

"THE GREATEST DISCOVERY OF MY GENERATION IS THAT A HUMAN BEING CAN ALTER HIS LIFE BY ALTERING HIS ATTITUDES."
——————— WILLIAM JAMES ———————

Everything that happens in college (in life, really) is both a lesson and a test. Your best bet is to treat all of it as an opportunity to learn and grow.

Don't pack it in when the bell rings! You're paying at least four years of your life and thousands of dollars to be here; milk it! Everything is a lesson in one way or another. You just have to have the right attitude.

"CHANGE IS NOT A FOUR LETTER WORD, BUT OFTEN YOUR REACTION TO IT IS."
——————— JEFFREY GITOMER ———————

Worrying, complaining and being negative or judgmental is a great way to waste time. Not only does it take a lot of energy, it never actually accomplishes anything, and it makes you feel worse, too. Look for the upside and find the lesson, instead!

"NOTHING IS A WASTE OF TIME IF YOU USE THE EXPERIENCE WISELY."
AUGUSTE RODIN

You crashed your bike and scraped your elbows?

You have two choices:

Freak out!
Worst day ever!
Sue whoever put
that pole there!

OR

Learn to handle this
minor crisis. It's just
practice for handling
a real one later.

You failed your test?

shrug it
off & move
on

OR

ask the
teacher
for answers/
help

Your professor is droning on about nothing?

_____
_____
_____
_____

OR

_____
_____
_____
_____

You have 300 pages of reading for tomorrow?

leave it to
the last
minute

OR

get a
head
start

Craig never loses, he either wins or learns...

Even if he wins, he learns how to do it better! He's always looking for the lesson.

Be like Craig.

What would Craig do?

WHAT LESSONS HAVE YOU LEARNED FROM SOME OF YOUR MOST NOTABLE WINS AND LOSSES?

"IT IS BETTER TO CONQUER YOURSELF THAN TO WIN
A THOUSAND BATTLES. THEN THE VICTORY IS YOURS.
IT CANNOT BE TAKEN FROM YOU, NOT BY ANGELS OR
BY DEMONS, HEAVEN OR HELL."
BUDDHA

Silly people

HAVE TO MAKE ALL THEIR MISTAKES THEMSELVES.

WHAT ARE SOME OF THE MOST MEMORABLE MISTAKES YOU'VE MADE? WHAT DID YOU LEARN?

Smart people

ALSO LEARN FROM OTHER PEOPLES' MISTAKES!

WHAT ARE SOME OF THE BIGGEST MISTAKES PEOPLE AROUND YOU HAVE MADE? WHAT CAN YOU LEARN FROM THEM?

LET IT GO!

Scientists offered a monkey a coconut that was far too large to fit through the bars in the monkey's cage. Nonetheless, the monkey grabbed and held onto that coconut for dear life. Even when the scientists put more food **inside** his cage on the other side, the monkey would absolutely not let go of the coconut that he would never even taste.

Often, you have to let go of what you know, your regrets or your "right to be right" so you can turn around and find something even better.

> "SOME OF US THINK HOLDING ON MAKES US STRONG; BUT SOMETIMES IT IS LETTING GO."
> HERMANN HESSE

Let go of trying to **look good**,
so you can actually **be good.**

There is such a thing as taking on too much. That's why you should be wary about committing to something before you're familiar with it and how it affects you. Try things and let them go if they don't fit. Go for what you really want!

WHAT ARE YOU HOLDING ONTO THAT MIGHT BE STOPPING YOU FROM GETTING SOMETHING EVEN BETTER?

WHAT'S YOUR COCONUT?

FORGET IT!

College is about learning new things... Duh! You might have "learned" something before, but be prepared to throw that right into the trash if you learn something that works even better. We're talking skills, techniques, beliefs, ideas, whatever.

> *"Those who cannot change their minds cannot change anything."*
>
> George Bernard Shaw

WHAT COULD YOU BENEFIT FROM LETTING GO? HOW WOULD IT
IMPROVE YOUR LIFE, AND WHAT WOULD IT COST YOU?

"IT'S EASY TO COME UP WITH NEW IDEAS; THE HARD PART
IS LETTING GO OF WHAT WORKED FOR YOU TWO YEARS
AGO, BUT WILL SOON BE OUT-OF-DATE."
ROGER VON OECH

CHALLENGE:

On the second day (not the first, it's too busy) of any course, go up to the professor and introduce yourself. Just express your feelings about the class and keep the conversation quick. Bada Boom! You're now a face with a name, not just another part of the crowd.

WHEN YOU THINK ABOUT ACTUALLY DOING THIS, HOW DO YOU FEEL? WHY DO YOU FEEL THAT WAY?

These two lines are the exact same size. Without adding anything to either, how do you make one line longer?

A _____

B _____

The answer is at the bottom of the page.

WHEN DO YOU FEEL LIKE YOU NEED TO SHOW OFF?
HOW DO YOU FEEL WHEN OTHER PEOPLE DO IT?

Answer: By making the other line shorter.

Live Like a
Professional Amateur

Make a habit of being the most curious, engaged and enthusiastic person in the room. Not only does it make for a more interesting life on your part, it is so uncommon among your peers that this simple habit will set you apart from the crowd immediately.

A crucial step in this process, though, is having the humility of the ideal amateur. Be open to being corrected, taught and guided and you will find people are very open to help, teach and guide you.

> "I AM THE WISEST MAN ALIVE, FOR I
> KNOW ONE THING, AND THAT IS THAT
> I KNOW NOTHING."
> SOCRATES

It's much better to look dumb and be smart, than be dumb and look smart.

Be Open!
Be Curious!
Be Uncertain!
Be Young!
Be Naïve!

WHAT PREVENTS YOU FROM DOING ANY OF THE ABOVE?

WATCH YOURSELF!

Do you feel like your emotions often control you? If you can learn to identify when your different emotions take charge, you can learn to work with them, instead of for them. One way to practice this is journaling! What a coincidence!

WHAT WERE SOME SIGNIFICANT TIMES WHEN YOU LET AN EMOTION CONTROL YOU? HOW DID THAT SITUATION TURN OUT?

GIVE NAMES AND FACES TO AS MANY OF YOUR MOODS AS YOU CAN
THINK OF. THEN WRITE DOWN A FEW WAYS TO IDENTIFY EACH OF
THEM WHEN THEY COME AROUND.

Examples: Furious Franklin. Ecstatic Ernesto.
Silly Susan. Depressive Donald. Manic Mandi.

.

What do $\boxed{\textbf{you}}$ want?

Making other people proud is nice, but it's important
to recognize the difference between living the way you
actually want to and living the way other people tell you
that you should want to.

A good way to tell the difference between something
you want and something you think you should want: if
you feel genuinely excited about a decision, it's probably
a good call. If your gut tells you something's off, trust it.

Also, check where you are when you make a decision.
Decisions made in manic or depressive moods usually
aren't a great call. Try to decide from a neutral state and
let all parts of you be part of the decision.

Tip: Don't make big decisions on the spot, especially
in front of somebody who has a stake in what you're
deciding on. The 'sleep on it' method is good, but I
would highly recommend the 'sleep, exercise, eat, talk
to some trusted (neutral) friends, eat, sleep again on it'
method for the really big stuff.

> "QUICK DECISIONS ARE UNSAFE DECISIONS."
> SOPHOCLES

64

WHAT EXCITES YOU? WHAT DO YOU FEEL PASSIONATE ABOUT? WHAT MAKES YOU FEEL ENGAGED AND INTERESTED? HOW CAN YOU STRUCTURE YOUR LIFE TO INCLUDE MORE OF THAT?

Open Up!

"Let go of certainty. The opposite isn't uncertainty. It's openness, curiosity and a willingness to embrace paradox, rather than choose up sides. The ultimate challenge is to accept ourselves exactly as we are, but never stop trying to learn and grow."

Tony Schwartz

When we hear things we don't like or agree with, we get upset or annoyed, but we are rarely open to take the time to sit down and explore why it is we don't agree with somebody or something. Try to leave your ego at the door and be open to other perspectives and ideas — you just might learn something.

"The trouble with having an open mind, of course, is that people will insist on coming along and trying to put things in it."

Terry Pratchett

There are situations where people will try to impose their beliefs on you, but you can remain open, without necessarily agreeing with everything you hear. Open means things can come in, but they can also go right back out.

You never know when or how your seemingly random knowledge and skills will come in handy. The best leaders have to be prepared for even the most unusual situation, and that means they have to be able to relate to anybody — even people with whom they strongly disagree.

Are you easily offended? *If* so, why do you think that is?
How do you feel about new ideas, people, etc.?
How could you benefit from being more open to new things?

Options for when you disagree:
"I've never thought of it like that!"
"That's an interesting idea!"
"I've never heard anyone put it quite like that!"

DON'T BE BUSY
GET BUSY!

Being busy is not an indication of success, it's a sign of poor planning.

Stressing out and being busy all the time is like running on a ship. It sure takes a lot of energy, but it doesn't get you where you're going any faster.

> "I'M KILLING TIME WHILE I WAIT FOR LIFE TO SHOWER ME WITH MEANING AND HAPPINESS."
>
> BILL WATTERSON

Do you consider yourself busy? Make a list of your obligations, responsibilities and must-dos. What are some other things you would rather do? Why?

A LACK OF TIME IS RARELY THE PROBLEM.
A LACK OF FOCUS OFTEN IS.

Avoid the "busy" trap. Cut the extra, useless stuff before you start talking about sleeping less, skipping meals, ditching the exercise routine or cutting class.

Facebook
Email
Texting
Youtube
Instagram
Snapchat
Twitter
Or whatever the heck

All cost WAY more time than you might think.

**The average Facebook user spends
<u>20 minutes</u> on the site per visit.**

How many times a day do you check Facebook?
And that's JUST Facebook.

Your time in college is an investment in your entire life. **There is no free time — it always costs you something else you could be doing.**

> "*TIME IS OUR MOST VALUABLE ASSET, YET WE TEND TO WASTE IT, KILL IT, AND SPEND IT RATHER THAN INVEST IT.*"
> JIM ROHN

Imagine this: Every morning you get $86,400 to spend however you want. But at the end of the day, it all goes away. No rollover, no exceptions.

Truth is, every morning you get 86,400 of something a lot more valuable: seconds. But we hardly ever think about **INVESTING** our time; we think about giving it away for free, wasting it, killing it or just spending it on junk.

How can you best invest your time in college, so you can see the best profits and enjoy it most?

*H*OW COULD YOU BETTER STRUCTURE YOUR WORK TIME
TO GET MORE DONE?

There are workflow gurus out there, like Tim Ferriss, who can give you specific, actionable plans to accomplish way more than you might think posssible, in way less time. Spend some time researching these things! It's worth it.

It's called a workFLOW, not a workCHOP.

You have to get into the flow of what you're doing, otherwise you're just wasting your time and energy.

Each time your workflow is interrupted by something like a text, side conversation or something of the like, it takes you a minimum of 10 minutes to really get back into the flow of doing whatever it is you're doing.

How much does a quick text really cost you?
Is that conversation worth sacrificing your goals?

STOP WORKING HARD.
START WORKING SMART!

College is as hard as you make it. It's much easier to be stressed out than it is to be calm, so naturally most people will tell you they had to fight their way through and stay up every night, freaking out about this or that. Don't do that.

Too much stress makes you stupid. When you're stressed out, your brain doesn't function at nearly the same level as it does when you are relaxed, calm and nourished. Think about it:

To your brain, stress = danger. In times of danger do you need to remember the chemical formula for blahblahblah or do you need to keep your body ready to run from something that might try to kill you? Any good brain will respond to high levels of stress by reducing higher functionalities of its own and giving that energy to the parts of the body that can keep you alive.

So, yes, by trying to work too hard all the time, you are making yourself stupid. Stop doing that! Start working smart, instead.

74

Stress, in mild doses, can be awesome and give you that little oomph to get things done. You just have to give yourself breaks every now and again. You can't run on turbo all the time — you'll burn out! And then what's the point of your perfect grades?

Remember the tortoise and the hare?
College is a marathon, not a sprint.

How do you manage times of stress? What are some techniques you've found to be effective? What are some that really are not effecive? When you look back, was most of your stress warranted or just a waste of time?

Get It Out of Your Head!

Write down your goals, obligations, desires, etc.

Research shows that just putting your goals on paper gives you a 50% higher chance of actually accomplishing them.

Once you've put your goals down, divide the task up into manageable chunks and get started!

Once you've gotten everything out of your head, you'll not only be more likely to actually get it all done, but you'll be much more able to relax and skip the stress because your mind won't constantly be working on it.

> "IF YOU HAVE A GOAL, WRITE IT DOWN. IF YOU DO NOT WRITE IT DOWN, YOU DO NOT HAVE A GOAL — YOU HAVE A WISH."
>
> STEVE MARABOLI

WHAT ARE THE FIRST GOALS, DESIRES AND OBLIGATIONS THAT COME TO YOUR HEAD? HOW CAN YOU MAKE THEM WORK WITH ONE-ANOTHER? TRY TO CLEAR YOUR MIND!

If you ever feel overwhelmed by how "busy" you are, take a few moments (on the toilet or whatever) and make a list of all your obligations. Then go back and rank those in terms of their fatality.

10 = I will actually, physically die if I don't do this.
1 = This is something I don't need to do, although I might want to.

The List

Do the 10s first and work your way down. The reality is, we can't do everything at once. But we can do something at once.

In times of stress, challenge, anger, fear, etc. imagine that somebody who you look up to is standing right by your side. That can often give you the boost you need.

WHO DO YOU LOOK UP TO? WHY? WHO IS SOMEONE THAT MIGHT LOOK UP TO YOU? HOW DOES IT HELP YOU TO THINK OF THEM WHEN YOU'RE IN TIMES OF STRESS?

Hint: Consider all the people you pass by in a given day. Do you think that one of them might be affected by your smile, or by something you do, like picking up a stray piece of trash?

Set Your Deadlines Before Anyone Else's

Being on time, if not early, is crucial. Whether it's turning in an assignment or going to a class, meeting, date, interview, etc. being on time is more than just a sign of respect, it's a reflection of your ability to plan and take responsibility. Keep yourself accountable to a schedule that you feel you can manage.

"EIGHTY PERCENT OF SUCCESS IS SHOWING UP."
ESPECIALLY IF YOU'RE ON TIME!
WOODY ALLEN

TIP: SCHEDULE YOUR DUE DATES AT LEAST ONE DAY BEFORE THE ACTUAL DUE DATE. SHOOT TO BE AT LEAST 15 MINUTES EARLY TO ANY SERIOUS MEETING, TEST, INTERVIEW, ETC. FIVE MINUTES EARLY IS FINE FOR SOCIAL MEETINGS.

IF YOU'RE LATE WITH ASSIGNMENTS OR TO MEETINGS OR APPOINTMENTS, WHAT IS YOUR GO-TO EXCUSE? HOW CAN YOU TAKE RESPONSIBILITY FOR YOUR SCHEDULE? WHAT ARE SOME WAYS YOU CAN PLAN IN ADVANCE TO MAKE SURE YOU'RE ALWAYS ON TIME?

DON'T BE THE BEST IN YOUR CLASS AT MAKING EXCUSES.

FIVE-STEP FORMULA FOR SUCCESS:

1. Identify business that needs to be taken care of.

2. Set a reasonably attainable goal for how much of said business you want to accomplish in 45 minutes.

3. Spend 45 minutes taking care of business without interruption. (That means no texting, facebook, talking, getting coffee, etc.)

4. Follow this with 15 minutes of stretching, checking your phone, chatting, whatever.

5. Repeat until business is taken care of.

You can focus on something for 45 minutes, can't you?

Take strategic breaks! Your mind and body need breaks every now and again if you want them to perform at their best #science.

Tip: Breaks happen BETWEEN periods of getting stuff done. It's not a break if you're always on it.

TRY THIS! WRITE A SCHEDULE FOR YOURSELF IN THE MORNING, INCLUDE SOME BREAKS AND WATCH HOW YOU MAGICALLY SEEM TO GET SO MUCH MORE DONE.

Pick Your Priorities!

A professor placed a jar on the podium at the head of his class. He filled the jar with rocks and asked his class, "Raise your hand if you think this jar is full." Almost everyone in the class raised a hand.

The professor then took out a bag of pebbles and poured it into the jar, where they fell between the rocks. "How about now?" Again everybody raised their hand. Once again, the professor brought out another bag, this time full of sand. After the sand had settled around the pebbles and the rocks, the professor asked again, "Is this jar full?" Everyone raised the hand once again, thinking it couldn't possibly go any further.

Then the professor emptied a water bottle into the jar. "Now, it's full. But how do you think this would have gone if I'd started with the water? Or the sand?"

Life is like that, too. If you start by taking care of the big, important things, all the rest will find a way to work itself in. But if you start with the little things, your big things aren't going to fit.

84

WHAT ARE SOME OF YOUR ROCKS? PEBBLES? SAND? WATER?
HOW CAN YOU MORE EFFECTIVELY PLAN YOUR DAYS
TO TAKE CARE OF THE ROCKS FIRST?

If you're going to study with somebody, make sure you're on the same page about getting stuff done. If your friend wants to have some casual time to chat and hang with you, do coffee instead.

> "IT IS NOT SO IMPORTANT TO BE SERIOUS AS IT IS TO BE SERIOUS ABOUT THE IMPORTANT THINGS. THE MONKEY WEARS AN EXPRESSION OF SERIOUSNESS WHICH WOULD DO CREDIT TO ANY COLLEGE STUDENT, BUT THE MONKEY IS SERIOUS BECAUSE HE ITCHES."
> ROBERT M. HUTCHINS

If you're going to study with someone, choose someone who you can **work** with, not just talk to.

The line between studying and hanging out is blurry.

WHAT ARE SOME WAYS TO MAXIMIZE THE EFFECTIVENESS OF YOUR STUDY TIME? DOES IT HELP YOU TO STUDY WITH FRIENDS, OR IS IT JUST A CRUTCH TO MAKE IT MORE ENJOYABLE? WHICH FRIENDS HELP YOU LEARN MORE AND WHICH JUST TAKE YOUR ATTENTION? WOULD YOU BE HAPPIER TO SOCIAL-STUDY FOR TWO HOURS, OR STUDY HARD FOR AN HOUR AND THEN SOCIALIZE FOR AN HOUR?

You want to be the best?
Then you have to do things in a
BETTER & SMARTER
way than everybody else.

> "*DON'T LOWER YOUR GOALS TO THE LEVEL OF YOUR ABILITIES. INSTEAD, RAISE YOUR ABILITIES TO THE HEIGHT OF YOUR GOALS.*"
>
> SWAMI VIVEKANADA

WHAT HABITS DO YOU HAVE THAT REALLY PUSH YOU TOWARD YOUR GOALS? WHAT HABITS DISTRACT YOU? WHAT NEW HABITS CAN YOU REPLACE YOUR DISTRACTING HABITS WITH?

Get Some Sleep!

Do you think athletes stay up practicing all night before the big game? No way! That would be ridiculous! Well, so is pulling an all nighter before your big test. Be smart!

1. Sleep makes you smarter.
2. Sleep can help you lose fat.
3. Sleep can improve your athletic performance.
4. Sleep reduces stress.
5. Sleeping more helps you live longer.
6. Sleep makes you more creative.
7. Sleep puts you in a good mood.

So be happy and choose to snooze!

How do you feel after a good night's sleep? How do you feel after staying up all night? Was the night worth not feeling so good the next day? Do you feel like you can perform how you want to on half the sleep?

"Sleep faster! We need the pillow!"

Sign in a hotel

WHAT YOU DO TODAY LAYS THE FOUNDATION FOR WHAT YOU CAN DO TOMORROW. HOW CAN YOU MAKE THE BEST USE OF TODAY TO SET YOURSELF UP FOR THE BEST POSSIBLE TOMORROW?

"*If you don't know where you're going, any road will get you there.*"

Lewis Carroll

Really, no road will take you there...

BLAZE YOUR OWN TRAIL!

There is a sect of monks high in the mountains, and they are absolutely not allowed to touch women – it is the foundation of their beliefs. One day, the head of the monastery was out walking with his apprentice when they come across an old woman struggling to cross a river.

Noticing her frustration, the master picked her up and carried her across to the other side. After a hearty thank you, the old woman continued on her way with a smile on her face.

The master and his apprentice arrived back at the gates of the monastery after a day's travel, and the apprentice said, "Master, I'm sorry, but I just can't believe you would go and carry that woman! It goes against everything we believe!"

The master smiled and replied, "Son, I carried that woman in my arms for a few minutes to help ease her struggle. For what purpose have you been carrying her in your mind all day?"

Fearing judgment or failure is like fearing your shadow. It's always going to find its way to you, somehow. So you might as well get used to it. Even better, learn to embrace and play with it!

> "WELL, LADDIE, IF YOU'VE LET AN OLD BUZZARD LIKE ME HURT YOUR CONFIDENCE, YOU COULDN'T HAVE HAD MUCH IN THE FIRST PLACE."
>
> TAMORA PIERCE

DO YOU WORRY ABOUT WHAT OTHERS THINK OF YOU AND YOUR DECISIONS? WHY? WHAT DIFFERENCE DOES IT MAKE, SO LONG AS YOU ARE COMFORTABLE WITH YOUR LIFESTYLE AND CHOICES?

If you can't get comfortable with rejection and failure, how do you expect to be comfortable with success, when those two might only be a second away? How can you define success for yourself in a healthy way?

People who are successful have often gone through huge failures to get there, but the difference is they **persevered**.

*Don't worry about what people think.
Most of the time – they don't.*

Post Failure Fix-Up!

1. Take a Deep Breath
2. Look for a Lesson
3. Learn Something
(if nothing else, to not do it again)
4. Move on!

You might find that when you get comfortable with taking risks, you strike gold.

One of the most notoriously difficult professors at a top university had never given an A on a test. As his final approached, his students were going mad with anxiety.

Finally, on the day of the test, the professor passed out a test with only one question on it.

Most students hung their head, resigned to the "F" that was imminent. One student, though, looked at the test, giggled, jotted down a couple words and turned in his test after about a minute.

The professor scoffed at the student's arrogance and snatched the paper from him. After reading the answer, though, the professor burst into laughter and immediately gave the student a perfect score.

The question: "What is courage?"
The answer: "**This is**."

WHAT RISKS HAVE YOU TAKEN IN YOUR LIFE? HOW HAVE THEY PAID OFF? WHAT TYPES OF RISKS ARE YOU COMFORTABLE WITH TAKING AND NOT TAKING? HOW CAN YOU DO THAT IN A WAY THAT PUSHES YOU TOWARD YOUR GOAL?

"IT'S BETTER TO BE ABSOLUTELY RIDICULOUS
THAN ABSOLUTELY BORING."
MARILYN MONROE

Make Friends!

Building relationships is the cornerstone of success. No matter what kind of grades you have on your transcript, if you can't relate to people, your chances of getting past an interview are close to zero.

> "*There are no strangers here; Only friends you haven't yet met.*"
>
> William Butler Yeats

Developing a genuine interest in others is an important factor in creating good relationships. But when we get caught up in the daily "busyness," we get self-centered, and start to look at other people as competitors or distractions, rather than potential friends or allies.

Do you feel it is easy or challenging to make friends? What do you feel are your biggest advantages and disadvantages when it comes to making friends? How can you improve?

"If civilization is to survive, we must cultivate the science of human relationships — the ability of all peoples, of all kinds, to live together, in the same world at peace."

Franklin D. Roosevelt

You never know the good a simple smile can do. You just might change someone's entire life by reminding them that there actually are things to smile about. Even if it means nothing to you, it might mean everything to them.

You want to be liked, respected and loved?

Like, respect and love others.

> "I SPEAK TO EVERYONE IN THE SAME WAY, WHETHER HE IS THE GARBAGE MAN OR THE PRESIDENT OF THE UNIVERSITY."
>
> ALBERT EINSTEIN

You want to be happy, successful and noteworthy?

Find ways to make other people feel happy, successful and noteworthy.

" ~~What~~ do you want to ~~do~~ when you grow up?"
Who   be

Research shows that social connections are one of the biggest predictors of success, happiness, health and general wellbeing. And, usually, they're a lot of fun. **But a big question is, how do you find the right people to connect with? Where are all the ones that share your interests?**

Try this: Pick something you're interested in and plug it into the highly scientific formula below! I can almost guarantee you'll find a club or class nearby with people who are interested in the same thing.

_____ + _____

(name of university)

(name of something you want to learn)

Who would've guessed?

P.S. if you don't find the thing you're looking for, create it! Somebody has to.

Break out of your comfort zone!
Success rarely hides in there with you.

WHAT ARE SOME PLACES, CONTEXTS, ORGANIZATIONS, ETC. THAT YOU
THINK WOULD HELP YOU MEET SOME NEW, INTERESTING PEOPLE?
WHAT KIND OF PEOPLE DO YOU HOPE TO FIND THERE?

Talk to Me!

It's not always easy to understand how to best connect with people, even once you've found people you're interested to get to know. Here are some quick tips:

Everybody's favorite subject is themself. You don't always have to have something to say, it's often better if you have something to ask, or even just show an interest in something they are wearing or doing.

Easy Conversation Starters:

Genuine (non-creepy compliments) like:
I really dig your watch, what kind is it?

I thought you had a really good point in class, how did you come up with that?

Points of commonality:
I noticed we're in the same section for Econ. What do you think of the professor?

Hey I like the hat! I grew up a big fan of the Dodgers, too. Are you from LA?

HOW DO YOU FEEL WHEN SOMEONE NEW TRIES TO TALK TO YOU?
DO YOU OFTEN TRY TO TALK TO PEOPLE WHO YOU DON'T KNOW?
WHAT DO YOU THINK IS AN EFFECTIVE WAY TO START A
CONVERSATION?

"ANY FOOL CAN CRITICIZE, CONDEMN AND
COMPLAIN. AND MOST FOOLS DO."

BENJAMIN FRANKLIN

If you can't hear what people want, need or desire, how are you going to be able to deliver that? If you can't hear what people are talking about, interested in or put off by, how are you going to be able to connect with them?

Well, in short, **you're not**.

"I FEAR THE DAY TECHNOLOGY WILL SURPASS HUMAN INTERACTION. THE WORLD WILL HAVE A GENERATION OF IDIOTS."

ALBERT EINSTEIN

Talk Small.
Listen Big!

The art of conversation – that is, listening and responding – is quickly being lost in the era of electronic communication.

One simple way to set yourself apart from the crowd is to ditch the phone and actually pay attention to the people around you, physically. Sounds dumb, but you'd be amazed how many people can't make it through a conversation without checking the phone.

ARE YOU ONE OF THEM?
ARE YOU A GOOD LISTENER?
HOW COULD YOU BE BETTER?

An old man hobbled into the doctor's office. The doctor examined the old man and said, "Sir, you should be very careful. You've got a heart murmur."

The old man suddenly perked up and said, "No problem!"

As the old man eagerly strolled out the door, the doctor scratched his head in wonder.

A few weeks later, the doctor saw his patient walking down the street looking 20 years younger, with a beautiful woman in his arm. The doctor walked up to him and said, "Good god, man! You look incredible. What happened?"

The old man replied, "I just followed your advice, doc!"

"And what was that advice, exactly?" the doctor wondered.

"You said, 'Be very cheerful and get a hot momma!'"

"IT'S A RARE PERSON WHO WANTS TO HEAR WHAT HE DOESN'T WANT TO HEAR."
DICK CAVETT

Who do you like / dislike listening to?
What is it they do? How can you learn from them?

We all like to feel heard. When we feel that way, it not only makes us feel good about ourselves, but also about the people listening to us!

_____

That's enough about me.

Let's talk about you.

What do you think about me?

_____

Tip: A key part of listening is hearing when it's your turn to spark the conversation, whether it's by engaging with what's being said, showing support or expressing some enthusiasm.

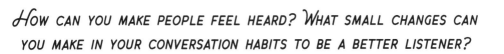

How can you make people feel heard? *What* small changes can you make in your conversation habits to be a better listener?

"*Most* people do not listen with the intent to understand; they listen with the intent to reply."

Steven R. Covery

It's easy to get stuck in the habit of spreading drama.

There was a famous experiment where scientists put five monkeys into a cage with a ladder. At the top of the ladder, the scientists placed a banana. When a monkey climbed the ladder, the scientists would pour cold water all over the other monkeys. After a while, the monkeys began to beat any monkey that tried to climb the ladder.

Then, the scientists swapped out one of the original monkeys with a new monkey. This new monkey tried to climb the ladder only to get beaten by the other monkeys. After a few days, the scientists switched out another monkey and found that the monkey who had never even seen the cold water fall would help to beat the new ladder-climbing monkey simply because he had beaten for it, himself.

At the end of the experiment, there were five new monkeys who had never experienced the water falling on them, yet they all beat any monkey who tried to climb the ladder because that is what they had been taught, without ever knowing exactly why.

"SO MANY PEOPLE PREFER TO LIVE IN DRAMA BECAUSE IT'S COMFORTABLE. IT'S LIKE SOMEONE STAYING IN A BAD MARRIAGE OR RELATIONSHIP - IT'S ACTUALLY EASIER TO STAY BECAUSE THEY KNOW WHAT TO EXPECT EVERY DAY, VERSUS LEAVING AND NOT KNOWING WHAT TO EXPECT."

ELLEN DEGENERES

Ditch the Drama!

In 5 years, you will not care whether that guy at the bar hit on your girlfriend, Sally texted your crush, Timmy blocked you into the driveway or even, really, what you got on that seemingly all-important test or essay. Why spend so much energy and emotion stressing about it now?

> "CONFLICT CANNOT SURVIVE WITHOUT
> YOUR PARTICIPATION."
> WAYNE DYER

When the drama kicks up
– and it inevitably will –
just kick it right back!

> "ADVERSITY HAS THE EFFECT OF ELICITING TALENTS, WHICH IN
> PROSPEROUS CIRCUMSTANCES WOULD HAVE LAIN DORMANT."
> HORACE

A little time, distance and perspective can save you a lot of pain and suffering.

> *"When things go wrong, don't go with them."*
> Elvis Presley

What dramas are taking room in your life,
and how do these dramas steal your energy?
How could you deal with them and move on?

Everyone likes to play the Drama Queen sometimes...
ALLOW YOURSELF THIS PAGE TO EXAGGERATE AND DRAMATIZE SOMETHING YOU FEEL STRONGLY ABOUT! REALLY GO FOR IT! MAKE IT SPICY!

When you focus on something, you attract more of it.
If you don't want more drama in your life, don't focus
on the drama around you.

WHAT IS SOMETHING YOU WOULD RATHER FOCUS ON AND ATTRACT?

It's much easier to remove yourself from drama when you feel like it's just somebody putting on a show. Their shows usually aren't very good, anyway – there are much better ones on Netflix.

Just watch yourself so you don't stoop to someone else's level. They're trying to get you to come play with them down there because, well, who wants to do a show all alone? If they get you to join them, who really wins?

You don't have to be a part of anyone's drama (including your own) unless you choose to.

"*IDENTITY IS PART OF DRAMA TO ME.*
WHO AM I, WHY AM I BEHAVING THIS
WAY, AND AM I AWARE OF IT?"
MATTHEW WEINER

WHAT BRINGS OUT THE DRAMA QUEEN IN YOU? AND WHO ELSE DO YOU LET PUT DRAMA IN YOUR LIFE? HOW CAN YOU AVOID IT?

THE WISE MAN
HELPS THE FALLEN ELEPHANT

It's important to be a good friend and help others, but it's equally important to know when to step out of someone's way to let them learn their own lessons. **Many of us don't learn until it hurts**.

THE STUPID MAN
TRIES TO STOP THE ELEPHANT FROM FALLING

WHAT ARE SOME SITUATIONS WHERE, OR PEOPLE WHO YOU TRY TO HELP A LITTLE TOO MUCH? HAVE YOU EVER BEEN DRAGGED INTO A SITUATION THAT WAS NEVER REALLY YOURS?

BE A SUPERHERO!

You want to be successful, powerful and loved like a superhero? Choose to be one! Step up when other people won't. Choose to be unshakeable. See solutions. **See ways to help others, not beat them.** Choose to do, handle and overcome the things most people don't dare to.

> *"YOU CAN TELL THE SIZE OF A MAN BY THE SIZE OF THE THING THAT MAKES HIM MAD."*
> *ADLAI STEVENSON*

It's picking up trash just because.
It's giving out compliments for the heck of it.
It's walking around with a smile on your face .
It's standing up for what you know is right.
It's living like your actions (and inactions) matter, for good or otherwise.

> "YOU CAN EASILY JUDGE THE
> CHARACTER OF A MAN BY HOW
> HE TREATS THOSE WHO CAN DO
> NOTHING FOR HIM."
> *MALCOLM FORBES*

WHAT IS YOUR SUPER POWER?
WHEN HAVE YOU BEEN A SUPERHERO?
WHAT SITUATIONS DO YOU REALLY SHINE IN?
HOW CAN YOU BE SOMEONE PEOPLE LOOK UP TO?

Expect the Black Swan.

In the old days, people used to say swans could never be black.

"Are you kidding me? Swans are white... stupid!"

Then, guess what? Someone found a black swan. Ever since, the expression has meant, "Something that everyone thought was impossible until it happened."

> "BE OPEN TO WHAT COMES NEXT FOR YOU. YOU MAY BE HEADING IN ONE DIRECTION AND THEN LIFE BRINGS YOU ANOTHER THAT MIGHT BE A GOOD THING."
> NATALIE CANE

Just because most people don't believe something is possible, does NOT mean you should agree with them. If you want to do something new, chances are most people don't think it's possible or a good idea. If they thought it was, they probably would have done it and then it wouldn't be there for you to do.

Other peoples' limitations are your opportunities.

IMAGINE FOR ONE MOMENT THAT YOU COULD DO, EXPERIENCE, FEEL AND HAVE ANYTHING YOU WANTED. WHAT WOULD YOU CHOOSE? HOW WOULD YOUR DAYS LOOK? HOW WOULD YOUR LIFE LOOK?

> *"If we only wanted to be happy, it would be easy; but we want to be happier than other people, and that is almost always difficult, since we think them happier than they are."*
> Charles de Montesquieu

At the end of your life what would like to say you accomplished? Why does your answer matter to you? Loosely, how do you plan to accomplish that?

> *"HE WHO HAS A WHY TO LIVE FOR CAN BEAR ALMOST ANY HOW."*
> *FRIEDRICH NIETZSCHE*

Often, we feel pressured by the expectations of family, society, school etc. to live and be a certain way, and it's easy to forget to stop and ask ourselves, "What do I really want? What is my passion?"

It's so easy to get tunnel vision. We're so busy answering questions like, "How do I get rich?" that we forget to ask the real questions like "Why am I here? What do I actually want to do with my life?"

> *"YOU CAN HAVE ANYTHING YOU WANT IF YOU WANT IT BADLY ENOUGH. YOU CAN BE ANYTHING YOU WANT TO BE, DO ANYTHING YOU SET OUT TO ACCOMPLISH IF YOU HOLD TO THAT DESIRE WITH SINGLENESS OF PURPOSE."*
> *ABRAHAM LINCOLN*

What's the use of being "successful" if you're stressed out, lonely and bored? If the price you're paying for success is unhappiness or bad health, are you really successful?

Without people to share success or money with, it's very hard to enjoy any of it.

If you don't like what you're doing now, what makes you think you're going to like doing what that leads to? Is it the fact that it might eventually get you paid?

After having enough money to survive, studies show that people don't actually gain any more happiness from having money.

Studies also show that people are happier when they are interested, engaged and invested in what they're doing. Passion > Money.

> *"The trouble with the rat race is that even if you win, you're still a rat."*
> *Lily Tomlin*

There are so many ways to be happy, experience the world and live the life you might dream of without money. **Look outside the box before you commit to living inside it.**

132

WHAT WOULD YOU CHOOSE TO DO IF MONEY, FAME AND RECOGNITION WERE NOT FACTORS? HOW WOULD YOUR DAYS LOOK? WHAT WOULD IGNITE YOUR PASSION?

"IF YOU LOVE YOUR WORK, YOU'LL BE OUT THERE EVERY DAY TRYING TO DO IT THE BEST YOU POSSIBLY CAN, AND PRETTY SOON EVERYBODY AROUND WILL CATCH THE PASSION FROM YOU - LIKE A FEVER."

SAM WALTON

133

A rich man saw a beautiful woman sitting at the bar across from him. Feeling a bit lonely, he walked up to her and said, "Would you sleep with me for a million dollars?"

"Wow… uh… sure!" The woman responded.

"How about for $100?"

"No way! Do you think I am a prostitute or something?"

"Well, we just established that. Now we're just negotiating the price."

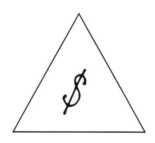

Selling out is easier than you think. The devil himself doesn't always come to your door and ask you to sign his big flaming scroll. It's usually much more insidious, like a great paying job that you hate or something your parents / friends want you to do that you really don't.

WHEN HAVE YOU SOLD OUT IN THE PAST BY AGREEING TO DO SOMETHING YOU REALLY DIDN'T WANT TO? DO NOTICE YOURSELF DOING IT WITH FRIENDS? FAMILY? WHO ELSE? WHAT STOPS YOU FROM SAYING NO?

The Minister of Leather

There once was a man named David Lee Briggs who ran a shoe shine station in the LAPD headquarters. This man was at his stand every single day, happily shining the shoes of the police department.

While the officers sat to have a shine, they would chat with the him about everything from stress on the job to problems at home. Just by lending an ear and some encouraging words, this man became one of the best parts of those officers' days. His shoe shines were fantastic, but the comfort and support he offered his customers was even greater.

When Briggs passed away, the LAPD didn't just mourn his death as a friend, they treated him as a real member of the force and gave him an honorable police funeral as a small thank you for his 21 years of service.

That is the power of going above and beyond in whatever job you have.

How can you put more passion into your daily life? What gets you excited? What bores you?

WOW!

Factor

The wow factor is that extra something that gives color to your life and makes you feel enthusiastic, energized and passionate. But how do you find yours?

> *"For the past 33 years, I have looked in the mirror every morning and asked myself: 'If today were the last day of my life, would I want to do what I am about to do today?' And whenever the answer has been 'no' for too many days in a row, I know I need to change something."*
>
> *Steve Jobs*

Before you invest a lot of your time, energy and resources into school or a career, it's well worth it to take a look at not only what you want to do and what you want to have, but who you want to **be**. Equally important as your to-do list, is your to-be list!

As a child, what did you dream about being as a grownup? Why do you think you loved that idea?

"Adults are always asking kids what they want to be when they grow up because they are looking for ideas."
Paula Poundstone

WHAT KIND OF LIFESTYLE DO YOU WANT TO LEAD?
WHAT ARE THE THINGS THAT MAKE YOU FEEL HAPPY?
TRAVELING? MONEY? SECURITY? CHALLENGES? TIME OFF?

"LIFE ISN'T ABOUT FINDING YOURSELF. LIFE IS ABOUT CREATING YOURSELF."
GEORGE BERNARD SHAW

How do you want people to tell your story?

"*If you would not be forgotten as soon as you are dead, either write something worth reading or do things worth writing.*"
Benjamin Franklin

141

Are you building your
BILLION-DOLLAR BRAND?

Think of it this way: You are in college to gain knowledge, of course, but also to start building your reputation. Once you accept that you are in control of how your "brand" develops (or stagnates) you can start taking steps to help yours stand out from the crowd.

WHO DO YOU ADMIRE? WHAT ABOUT THEM DO YOU FIND INSPIRING? WHAT DO THESE PEOPLE REPRESENT THAT YOU WOULD LIKE TO DEVELOP IN YOURSELF?

If you put your mind to it, you can be someone inspiring, too. But you might have to sacrifice a few things along the way... If it was easy, everyone would do it.

> *"Don't wait until you are big to start building your brand. Build a brand from scratch alongside your business."*
>
> Sir Richard Branson

What are you doing to be exceptional? What is unique about you? How can you use your unique experience, skills, features, dreams, background, etc. to set yourself apart?

We all have moments of greatness and moments of weakness, but what really counts is how you represent yourself and your brand on a day-to-day basis through your daily choices.

Of course, there are the exceptionally good moments that can make you a hero, and the exceptionally bad that can make you a villain. Those both tend to overshadow the day-to-day. Just stay away from the latter.

WHAT WOULD YOU DIFFERENTLY IF YOU COULD DO IT OVER? IF YOU EVER BECOME FAMOUS OR RUN FOR OFFICE, ARE THERE THINGS ABOUT YOU THAT YOU WOULD PREFER TO STAY PRIVATE? WITH THESE QUESTIONS IN MIND, HOW CAN YOU DO BETTER FROM HERE ON OUT?

"IT TAKES 20 YEARS TO BUILD A REPUTATION AND FIVE MINUTES TO RUIN IT. IF YOU THINK ABOUT THAT, YOU'LL DO THINGS DIFFERENTLY."

WARREN BUFFETT

According to a Yale physicist, it should be physically impossible to hit a Major League Baseball pitcher's fastball. It moves so quickly that, by the time the hitter should be able to see the ball, analyze its movement and swing, it should be far past them. Yet somehow, people hit fastballs all the time. How? They can visualize where the ball is going before it gets there, and they can see themselves hitting it.

Of course years of training help. But, if there's a doubt in that batter's mind, do you think that he has a chance of hitting a 97.5 MPH fastball? No way.

> "YOU CAN'T THINK AND HIT AT THE
>
> SAME TIME."
>
> YOGI BERRA

Think about this: the best batters in the world consistently hit the ball 3-4 times of 10 and that makes them superstars.

Believe in yourself, even if you mess up every now and again.

> "I HAVE NOT FAILED. I HAVE JUST FOUND
>
> 10,000 WAYS THAT WON'T WORK."
>
> THOMAS EDISON

WHAT MAKES YOU NERVOUS? WHAT DON'T YOU BELIEVE YOU CAN DO? HOW CAN YOU PUSH PAST THOSE LIMITATIONS?

"ADVERSITY CAUSES SOME MEN TO BREAK; OTHERS TO BREAK RECORDS."

WILLIAM ARTHUR WARD

Quiet Your Mind!

Creating time for some form of prayer, contemplation or meditation is one of the things most successful people have in common. Whether it's taking a quiet walk on the beach, a yoga class or even just sitting by yourself for a few minutes, the key is to create some quiet time in the middle of even the craziest day.

"It takes a lot of time to be a genius. You have to sit around so much, doing nothing, really doing nothing."
— Gertrude Stein

Quick Tip: Take 5 minutes today and focus on your breathing. Listen to yourself and your body and nothing else. If your mind wanders too much, count your breaths, or search the web for meditation videos.

WHAT MIGHT BE AN EFFECTIVE METHOD OF MEDITATION FOR YOU?
COULD YOU DEDICATE 5 MINUTES PER DAY TO TRY
MEDITATING, OR AT LEAST JUST SITTING QUIETLY?
IF YOU FEEL STRESSED BY THAT IDEA, WHY IS THAT?

HAVE A VISION!

Some may insist that visualization is just dreaming, but it's actually being taught by major consulting firms to some of the most powerful people in the world. Plus, think of it this way, our lives would be very different if people had not dreamt about things like electricity, cars, internet and computers...
So, even if it is like dreaming, what's the problem?

> "LOGIC WILL TAKE YOU FROM A TO B.
> IMAGINATION WILL TAKE YOU EVERYWHERE."
> ALBERT EINSTEIN

Create a very clear, specific vision of what you want, feel it as if it has already taken place and make sure to bring it to life with as much positive emotion as you can. Every chance you get, add some enthusiasm to keep your vision alive.

This will create a blueprint for your future and help you focus on the prize, not the problems. Keep that feeling and that image in your mind to block out stress and anxiety. Positive Visions = Positive Results.

TAKE A FEW MOMENTS TO VISUALIZE YOUR PERFECT FUTURE. WHO WOULD BE IN IT? WHERE WOULD YOU BE? WHAT WOULD YOU BE DOING? HOW WOULD YOU FEEL? HOW WOULD YOU ACT? ETC. DESCRIBE IT IN AS MUCH DETAIL AS POSSIBLE.

Give Back!

Part of being successful is giving back. Today we often talk about carbon footprints, but it's also important to think about what kind of positive footprint you create.

Start with something small: give a friend a few extra minutes of your time instead of rushing off, give someone a little extra attention if you see they aren't feeling great or just smile because you can.

IS THERE A CAUSE YOU FEEL STRONGLY FOR?
IS THERE A DIFFERENCE YOU WOULD LIKE TO MAKE?
WHAT DO YOU WANT YOUR LEGACY TO BE?

"WHETHER YOU LIVE TO BE 50 OR 100
MAKES NO DIFFERENCE, IF YOU MADE NO
DIFFERENCE IN THE WORLD."
JAROD KINTZ

CREATE YOUR OWN PORTABLE PARADISE!

You have the power to make your own paradise, wherever you go and whatever you do.

This sounds great on one hand, but it puts quite a bit of responsibility on your shoulders because nobody else can do it for you.

As you go through your college career, pay attention to the things that make you feel like you're in paradise.

Is it being surrounded by friends? Is it the variety of opportunities? Is it the environment? Is it that feeling when you helped someone and saw their face light up?

Whatever it may be, keep it in mind as you design the rest of your life.

Every chapter comes to an end, but the story goes on. A lot of people in college have a little nagging voice in their head saying, "You'll never have it this good again." Well, my final challenge to you is this: **make sure it only gets better from here.**

Try to understand yourself: what you love, who you love, what you need, where you need to be, what you need to do, and all of that good stuff. And just let it change as it does. Let it come in and roll right back out just like waves.

Be kind, open and patient, find your passion, keep stumbling forward and, most of all, have and spread joy wherever you go and whatever you do.

If you can do that, you can be the most successful person in the world, even without having a dollar to your name, but I bet you'll have plenty of dollars, too.

Thank You!

If you are interested in more than just Pocket Coaching, We are available for consulting, too! For more information, or to share some feedback or thoughts...

Please email me at
Info@PeacefulViking.com
and check out
Peacefulviking.com

I would love to hear from you :)

You've Made Your Coach Very Proud!

Made in the USA
San Bernardino, CA
02 September 2016